Love Songs for a Tender God

Love Songs
for a Tender God

Hiro Boga

OOLICHAN BOOKS
LANTZVILLE, BRITISH COLUMBIA, CANADA
2002

National Library of Canada Cataloguing in Publication Data

Boga, Hiro, 1949-
 Love songs for a tender god

 Poems.
 ISBN 0-88982-216-6

 I. Title.
PS8553.O464L68 2002   C811'.6   C2002-910283-9
PR9199.4.B63L68 2002

The Canada Council | Le Conseil des Arts
for the Arts | du Canada

We gratefully acknowledge the support of the Canada Council for the Arts for our publishing program.

BRITISH
COLUMBIA
ARTS COUNCIL
Supported by the Province of British Columbia

Grateful acknowledgement is also made to the BC Ministry of Tourism, Small Business and Culture for their financial support.

Canadä

We acknowledge the financial support of the Government of Canada through the Book Publishing Industry Development Program for our publishing activities.

Published by
Oolichan Books
P.O. Box 10, Lantzville
British Columbia, Canada
V0R 2H0

Printed in Canada

To the moon reflected in many waters—
Jesse and James
Parvana and Nivedita
beloved friends

Acknowledgements

How does a writer thank the ground on which she stands? Without the love, encouragement and support of my teachers, family and friends, this book would be a house without a foundation, without walls or a roof.

My deepest gratitude to George McWhirter and Ron Smith, whose wisdom, skill and generous, patient help have profoundly shaped these poems.

Many thanks to Pat Smith, Jay Connolly, Maureen Connolly, and Linda Martin of Oolichan Books; Kate Braid and Steve Guppy, and colleagues at Malaspina University-College; Peggy Thompson and friends at the Creative Writing Department of the University of British Columbia.

And thanks beyond words to my spiritual teachers, including my father, Kobad Boga, Dorothy MacLean, David Spangler, Lingtrul Rinpoche and my sons, Jesse and James; my dear sisters, Parvana and Nivedita; and my miraculous friends, who show me every day what love is—Jan Bracewell, Michael Bruce, Ruth Campbell, Robin Chakravarti, Elizabeth Comtois, Louise, Renwick, Masae, Shifra and Haigan Day, Diane Denoon, Nancy Garnons-Williams, Thora Howell, Kelly Murphy, Liza Potvin, Judith Snider, Beth Taylor-Harris and Jacqueline Wareham.

Contents

I

Love Songs for a Tender God

SERENADE

Feet planted in mud, cinnamon silt and sand
I rise to you through wavering green water.
Through blooms of algae, tangled weeds, I rise
unfold in the arbour of your tendrilled sun.
I rise, sweet breath of life, to you.

I breathe your fragrant air. Rooted
in tangles of despair I rise, sweet singer,
to your song, and all my yearning
yields to the height, breadth
and depth of you. I rise, great bard, to you.

And in that meeting-place of pond and sky
my I dissolves in your light
boundless, boundless welcome.

ELEGY

When I bend and bind
squeeze my soul into narrow shoes,
deck it out in gaudy hues
of other peoples' clothing;
when I alter my inherent shape, strut
through attenuated alleyways of dialectic,
I lose you, crumble. I know
you are in me but I cannot reach you
in the rubble of my ignorance.

Such loneliness engulfs me
then, not all the soft-voiced friends, sultry
gongs of lust and wine assuage.
I am orphaned,
a lover bereft, a leather-shod beast without
breath, a vast homesick wail
in the wilderness:

I am homesick.

A CAPELLA

My life is bread-making.
Daily I work the dough.

My hands blend, shape it
into supple balls and then

I wait for your sacrament
of warm brown flour, sea-salt

water, a sprinkled
benediction,

to expand in me,
dissolving this mass

becoming
a fine leavening.

PRAYER

Let me embrace you
naked as rain.

Let all that is not me fall
away. This body drawn to earth's
molten heart, this mind echoing
your fingerprint, these avid ears

drinking your elemental voice.
Let me know you in clamouring
cities, viridian hills,
in curled fists of my child.

Let me embrace you
naked as rain.

PLAYMATE

When icy winds blow
when clouds lower, and storms

twist roots of sable trees
I bolt to you for shelter.

Your hand in mine slows
my heartbeat to steady

measure. I come fleeing to you
now in clement weather.

INVOCATION

In this moment is the grace
of your presence. Yet as your star

brings daybright light and life
to the manifest world, so these words
will flow from fingertips
onto this page—

veils drawn across this union.

You are that which moves and is moved,
wind that sets reeds singing
and dancing, ancient reed beds
that murmur and sway.

You this sun's ardent kissing
the rushing river, you the river of leaping.

Birdsongs ring the vault of heaven—
hawk and horizon, wind and wing, all you.

You the limpid sky across whose bowl
clouds tumble. You the nimbostratus pall
that precipitates. Cedar tree and earth,

the seed from which the embryo grows—
the slow turnings of gestation, are you.

The Pleiades, Andromeda, are the blazing
of your love. All worlds are you.

VOCALISES

1

Break
my heart

open
with the hammer

of your love.
Grind me

to powdered sand.
Blow me

on *khamsins*
of your breath

into the deserts
of the earth.

2

The sun
comes

smoothes
my shadow

into silk.
You

sculpt
my reflection

in gold.

3

Burn

until my candle
melts

in tongues of flame

burn in me.

4

I come to you empty,
mind and heart hollow.

Fill me
with the thrumming
of your presence.

5

My heart is fierce
longing. I am
the tumult of this world.
Bring me home. I lead to nothing
else. Where I go
you are.
No I, only
us.

6

Let me love you
as silence loves the seed of sound

As you love me

Let me love
as wave loves particle

As you love

Let me
as all is you

Be you

MEDITATIONS

&

bones glow
under lucent membrane

and the pulse. and the pulse.

the pulse, Beloved,
                    is you

In the centre of my heart is a
sun in whose warmth
apple trees blossom

In the centre of my heart is a chamber
through which the mistrals of heaven blow

In the centre of my heart
songbirds till a garden

In the centre of my heart is a
window through which a meadowlark
flies out

In the centre of my heart a living
pearl illumines the stars

In the centre of my heart emerald mountains
ring a sapphire lake

In the centre of my head is a rain-washed
dawning

In the centre of my head cirrus
clouds cross a cobalt sky

In the centre of my head a hermit thrush
sings sweet wilderness

In the centre of my head a bare room
opens into the fragrance of your hands

In the centre of my head is a mirror
in which your face is reflected

In the centre of my head is a wet beach
bearing the footprints of your love

In the centre of my crown an ocean laughs

In the centre of my crown a great blue heron
skims the rim of earth

In the centre of my crown
a cloud-wreathed peak
pierces the skin of eternity

In the centre of my crown is a
wooden ladder you climb
down to meet me
and I
climb up to meet you

In the centre of our crown is an orbit
of grace

a meadow of wildflowers
in which we lie down crushing woodviolets

In the centre of my throat is templed
silence

is a boat with billowing sails

a song that sings you; in the centre

of my throat is a deep well
from which you and I drink

a harvest moon in a hyacinth sky.

In the centre of my ribs, a silver salmon
leaps

In the centre of my ribs, a rock of granite
from earth to heaven

In the shelter of an oak a redwinged
blackbird
nests

In a viridian
pond, mallards teach
their ducklings to swim

In the centre of my ribs, an infant
breathes

an angel
with hair of green willow
in the centre of my ribs

In the centre of my belly a red arbutus
overleaps the edge of a cliff

In the centre of my belly a healing rain
widens the channels of a river as it flows
into the sea

In the centre of my belly a cradle of darkness
nurtures all life

In the centre of my belly a net of stars
flies across the tops of fir trees

In the centre of my belly dolphins play

In the centre of my womb, a resinous tree
with mango-laden branches

an angel of humour
who trades stories
with silly children

In the centre of my womb a tribe of dancers
twirls into being

In the centre of my womb a wilderness
whose name only you and I know

In the centre of my womb a deep cave
in which I kneel and kiss the source

II

He Who Puts God in his Mouth

TENEREMENTE

I stand at the boundary. On this side, familiar
terrain. Hills like lyric waves brushed with sage, dew
an aria on my tongue, golden wedge of light on my
elbow. My cradling arms know precisely my baby's
milky weight, his warm mouth loose against my
breast, my nipple cooling in this lambent dawn.
Moss furs nuzzle the soles of my feet.

This is the threshold: this granite arch soaring
skyward in the middle of a mustard field, keystone
lost in the limpid blue of heaven. I face unknown
country. Images pour through my head like rain:
Death in rusty black cloak, hooded, faceless, scythe
gripped in blanched fingers. And bodies, light as
dried laurel leaves, borne on bamboo biers, covered
in marigolds; tinkling cymbals, heartbeat of drums,
chanting voices bearing the soul back home.

That which is before me is veiled in light. My hand
through the archway no longer a hand, effulgence
of ultraviolet pulsing to a rhythm familiar as my
heartbeat, enigmatic as an atom. I lean my upper
body through the arch. Soft. Smell of almond
blossoms, sticky fig juice, olive groves. Shiver of
argent sound, bells, chiming inside and out into one,
my skin no longer my skin, no boundary, but a
dissolved definition. I exchange electrons and
protons with ambient life which once bore many
names—tree, fish, star, mud. My flesh and theirs

transmuted into vibration, dance of particles into
waves, waves and particles, call and answer, calando,
dolce, dolce, tranquillo. I am a sympathetic string in
a great aeolian harp, vibrating to the melody of these
rushing winds, vast ripples of light and air and spirit.

I step across the slate-grey stones. Prelude over,
my voice flows into this canon which sings the Real.
My infant son plays in the crack between worlds,
time in his right hand, eternity in his left. He puts
God in his mouth and savours, rolling divinity on
his tongue, face rapt, chortling his own cantata.

THE FEAST OF ST. THOMAS

"Love your brother as your soul; guard him as the pupil of your eye."
— The Gospel of Thomas

They come from far and wide these men and women,
carrying babies on their hips,
solemn in their Sunday best.
Scraggly lines of them shuffle along
to view my body in this open coffin where it has lain,
unblemished and immaculately preserved,
for two thousand years. That miracle
so impressed the pope, he proclaimed me a saint.
So they come, these fishermen and shopkeepers
housewives grandmothers murmuring
prayers, entreaties, bargaining with God.
Their prayers rise up to heaven, as smoke.

The air in this church is thick with incense, yellow
with the light of sulphurous candles lit
by these pilgrims for the souls of their dead.

Love your brother as your soul...

The Syrian Bishop of Kerala raises his arms
in blessing; purple robes and snowy mitre proclaim
his holy office. Thousands kneel to kiss his ring before
bending to kiss the feet of the body I left behind
so many centuries ago. Hundreds faint, unable to breathe
the close and humid air in St. Thomas's cathedral.

Imagine! They named a cathedral after me.
After me, Thomas, who never knew
where I'd rest my head at night
once I entered my Beloved's holy service.

Ah, but that was the joy of it! In my youth
I believed what my senses told me. If I couldn't
see taste touch smell or hear it
it didn't exist. I was sure of that. Until God demanded
everything I cherished most: my Beloved's sacred life
my livelihood my attachment to family friends security
home name country proof everything.

Everything.

I roamed the world and found my faith anew each day
as this family or that shared with me
whatever they had. Some nights I slept in royal chambers;
on others I was lulled to sleep by the whisper of the sea
as I laid my head in the sands of some foreign shore.

. . . guard him as the pupil of your eye.

When my time came to leave this mortal body, it was here
on the west coast of India, its southernmost tip,
in the lush and verdant plains of Kerala, that God demanded
my life. And I gave it, most gratefully, surrendering this
perplexing burden—God made human in me.

Every year since, on the anniversary of my death,
they wheel my coffin on its teakwood catafalque
out into the apse of this cathedral.
Thousands of prayerful pilgrims wait
to view my mortal remains, searching
in my miraculously uncorrupt body for a sign
that there is a God; that some Divinity has the power
to answer their prayers.

In this mass of sweating humanity my eye
catches glimpses of illuminati. This woman

in a brown cotton dress, holding her toddler
on her shoulders so the child may breathe

a clearer air; that ancient pushed
along in a makeshift wheelchair

by his rapturous grandson; and there
by the far wall an aging thief

washing his soul clean with tears
of repentance: each of them

bears the glow of inner knowing.
God is everywhere.

Walking up to the coffin, now, is a young man
so jittery, so uneasy in his skin,
that even in the press of this throng

he is set apart. The people near him
pull away, repelled by the aura of violence
he wears around him like a carapace. He edges
nearer the foot of the coffin; bends down,
as others do, brings his mouth to the relic's feet.
Then, sudden screams from the woman behind him
bring the ushers running. There are shrieks and cries
shouts and wailing all around. I look, and see blood
spurting from the right foot of my newly desecrated
body. The young man is kneeling, still, before the coffin
his eyes glazed, unseeing. Tears pour down
his sallow cheeks. The ushers grab him roughly
by his armpits, drag him to his feet. Blood
stains his chin; his mouth is clamped firmly
around the bleeding digit that is my severed big toe.
He has bitten it right off, in a transport of ecstasy
or indignation. And I am angry. This is all that's left
of my incarnation; witness to my terrible struggle with being
human. Now my body, twin and mirror of my Beloved's
own, is utterly defiled, fills the mouth of this hungry
stranger. Like the rumbling of an earthquake, then,
I hear God's loving laughter deep
in my soul: *One more thing, Thomas,*
I ask of you. Will you give it? Willingly? And I tussle
with my heart: "This is all I have left, Lord, why
would you ask this of me?"
And God's voice, rutilant with Divine joy: *I do ask it,*
Thomas. You are free to say yea or nay. What
will you do? My soul's answer rises, singing:
"Yes, my Beloved, yes, yes, and yes!" even while

this stubborn darkness in me growls, "I am a saint,
worthy of reverence. Punish this man."

I turn my gaze upon the sacristy. Uniformed
guards come rushing in. They shout questions, exclaim
angrily, wave their arms about. The crowd
presses in. The young man stands meek and amazed,
all the violence drained out of his soul. He says
nothing, bows lower as the voices around him rise
like the tide. The glow of illumination is upon him.
I can see, in his stillness, he hears nothing.
His ears are filled with the voice of God.

And I hear my own Beloved's voice, echoing
down the centuries, clear as water now, priceless
gift from this troubled man, my brother,
struggling, as I have done, to reconcile
those fractious twins, human divinity:

Love your brother as your soul,
guard him as the pupil of your eye.

ENTROPY

Lock the doors, bar the windows!
My house is under siege.

Roots of fir trees crack
the foundation. Dirt from the garden

drifts in. Moss lifts
shingles off the roof. Creosote

corrodes the chimney.
Black fungus crawls around the window

frames, devours bathroom walls.
Icy air needles through invisible crannies.

The furnace flickers
and dies.

The back porch is rotting into the ground. The lawn
is slick with moss.

The living room floor billows
and sags. Gyproc buckles under angry fists.

Lightbulbs flare like matches
and go out.

Cabinet doors fall off their hinges. Countertops
heave. Plumbing defies gravity.

Doorframes lean on a single nail.
The toothy munch of termites invades my sleep.

My husband says, "It's fine. You worry
too much." Ceiling plaster dusts his hair.

Maybe an earthquake will demolish this house.
Maybe a giant toe,

descending.

BUDDHIST CHRONICLES

1

Yashodhara & Siddhartha: The Parting

Would you leave me, Siddhartha? This bed,
its crumpled sheets still bear the imprint
of our bodies. Look, I will cut off my hair,
these heavy tresses you love to twine around your wrists;
I will lock my legs around your waist.
I will not let you go.

Will you leave me?

I left my father's orchards for you,
learned to love these echoing hills
because they are your home.
My only home is you.
I left them all: my mother, who wept at our wedding
like the Ganges in full flood; my father, brother,
the country of my birth.
I came to you bereft of language;
we spoke in whispers of blood, thunder of flesh
rejoicing. Do you remember? We made love
on the balcony until it broke and we fell,
still entwined, onto the ground below.

And now you tell me you must go?

You say you've looked into the entrails
of suffering and cannot rest until you know
how the story ends. Your mind trembled
when you met that unholy trinity:
sickness   old age   death.
But we are young, Siddhartha,
my belly leaps with new life. Stay.
Stay for your child
if not for me.

Why can you not stay? Does my beauty
unman you? Your mouth flutters like a bird
beneath my fingers and my heart shouts
in my chest and yet, the curve of my lips,
is it the entrance to death's cave?
Must you go?

2

Rejection

Don't preach to me, Siddhartha. You are an old man
who masquerades in a young man's clothes.
Don't talk to me of afterlife; I know what I know.
My body is my guide. Beat of pulse, belly's cry,
the raging of my thighs tell me all I need to know.
Your heavenly consolations are not for me.

Go to your hermit's cave, Siddhartha. Reject
the body's truths of blood and bone
for arid philosophical perfection.
Sultry night and all the burning stars will
bed with me when you are gone.

3

Rahula's Demand

Where is my father?
Why do you sit all day by the window
gazing out at the sky, and at this winding path
that leads away from our mountain kingdom?

Mother, come, play with me. I have a new monkey
with soft white fur, black rings around his eyes;
he speaks to me in monkey tongue,
tells me stories of the bazaar.

Why must I stay here in grandfather's palace?
It is pestilent with women and old men
hiding from the cold.

I want to see my father.
Take me to him.

4

Prajapati

I loved Siddhartha as my own
my sister's child, suckled
at my breast

but I saw him always
for what he was

a prince
shielded by garden walls.

He had never known death;
even the flowers in his orchards

were picked before their petals fell.
He never knew the stench of decay

or the rotting fruit
life vomits up.

Yasodhara was different;
she knew their happiness was fragile

a pale blue egg bravely held
in the hollow of her hand.

She fought for it

while he, who had never been denied
crushed it

in his fist.

And yet, he was tender,
an orchid sweetening this mountain air

his father's prize

he could have turned out spoiled as a peacock
all those palaces built for him, all those

dancing girls with naked breasts and
rubies gleaming in their pubic hair.

But he had a purity of heart that would not let him
sink into these pleasures. He was very young

when his cousin shot a swan and claimed it
as his trophy. Siddhartha drew the arrow from the bird's

bleeding breast, warmed her injured heart against his own,
nursed her till she healed
and flew away.

Still, he was a prince
raised to believe
the kingdom took wing from him.

Selfish in his way, as she in hers, he was all
clarity and air,
cool detachment;

she was earth, and water.

Asceticism.
Appetite.

And yet, they chose each other.

This is the secret that overflows
in her eyes.

I wasn't surprised when he left,
though I feared for Yasodhara's sanity.

5

Yasodhara's Lament

Tides of grief
through my veins

From this swollen heart into estuaries

I mourn the wrack
to come

I have stored pain like marrow
like treasure in the caves

of my bones

Bloodwaters crash and break
on this spiny shore

6

Suddhodana's Dilemma

The king sits in council
with his ministers. His heir
has vanished
choosing the ascetic's empty bowl
over the imperial crown.

Seven sages had predicted this
the day Siddhartha was born.
His would be a destiny of choice:
Emperor
or Enlightened One.

The king tried
to keep his heir at home. He buried
the writhing of the flesh
under garments of gold.
Ascetics were plentiful as leaves.
He had only one first-born son.

Now he wrinkles the imperial forehead.
Turns brusquely to his chief minister,
orders Prince Nanda to be brought
to the council chamber.

7

Siddhartha At The Boundary
Of The Sakya Kingdom

Moonless night; cloud
silk across lowering sky.

In my father's palace Yasodhara sleeps,
my son's newborn body curled against her breast:
a snail in its shell.

I have turned my trembling back
on all I love,

tethered still by ropes of desire,
longing. O heart

that hammers against the doors of the sky,
I creep forward to meet this cryptic night.

The river hisses, a cobra at my feet.
I can bear no more goodbyes.

I must make a fist of this heart.

Channa, take my clothes;
these silks and jewels chafe like a yoke.

Give them to my father. Tell him, I will return

when I have found the jewel I seek. Kanthaka,
you must gallop back to the palace too.

I cannot take you with me.

8

At The Boundary — The River Anoma

You stand on my northern bank,
a lacerated young man, with tender-soled feet.
Your tears prick my skin;
droplets of salt swirl in secret eddies.

Do you know what you invoke, O prince?
I am as wide as the chasm between lives.
My waters erase the known world.
My ways are ancient
and hard. I dwindle mountains into pebbles
round and smooth as pearls.
There is no immunity here.
Men have drowned in these currents.

You hack off your hair with a sword, leave it blowing
like straw on my flanks. But that which you sever
once you step into my belly
will bleed dark as rubies:
fearful, benevolent as death itself.

Loneliness will wear you down with the slow grinding
of millstones. Your mind will be drenched in fear
and hunger. You will twist in currents of longing
while fish nibble at your entrails.

Think well, before you enter my embrace.

9

Yasodhara

Yesterday
the magnolia's perfect bowl
brimmed with rain-water

Now, a single petal,
mottled cream and brown,
droops outward

The bowl is broken

Rahula runs towards me
his laughing face upturned

Two raindrops tremble
on the blossom's ivory lip

BODH GAYA

So this is where you sat,
having vowed not to move
until you'd grasped what you were looking for—
the root of human suffering.

To see things as they are. Girders
of life, architecture of light
underlying all creation. You met

demons, temptresses, your own
body's fearful trembling, heartbeat
slipping sideways into a crack of time
no bigger than a sliver, torso held upright
only by implacable will. So you sat,
vision turned inward, cross-legged
in the shade of this Bodhi tree. Emerged
at last from your long quest, simooms
blowing through the sockets of your eyes.

Stripped to the bones, this
is what you saw. All phenomena *anicca*—
impermanent as a flower,
death sprouting darkly with the seed.
Sunyata—emptiness—at the heart of all
being. You smiled,
offered a lotus blossom to your faithful disciple
in lieu of a doctrine.

Now, 2400 years later, an adamant temple
towers hundreds of feet into the dusty ochre sky
of Bodh Gaya. Carved with images of your face,
your serene smile repeated over
and over, ubiquitous as the Golden
Arches. Your radical discovery of nothingness
is surrounded now by an economic empire.

Priests, pilgrims, vendors of yak tea
and prayer flags. Rivers of gold empty
into temple coffers, young Tibetan monks
perform a hundred thousand prostrations
in the cobbled walkway,
kneepads and mittens cushioning the scrape
of shale on flesh. Enlightenment

without pain. And you smile, oh Buddha,
at these frantic stances on the rim
of the Great Void.

SAP RISING

And that sap, rising,
joyous in the noon air
while the root follows gravity.
One thrust
into the soil of work and family,
the raucous hum of the town's nights sliced through
proclaims the disorders of a wandering life.
Daughter to mother singing
purple east to dove-grey west.

A marriage bursts the springs of its ancient bed
and still, the sap rises.

In the garden,
green stems burred with velvet thorns
kiss the light, twist
skyward,
for a temperate sun, the chill of night.
Roots in frozen soil to a depth
of three feet and the faltering sap
flows in winter's sleep
and still   and slow   it rises.

III

I Lie Where
My Family's Hungers
Have Hatched Me

POST-MORTEM

This is my father's child, mother. My
half-sister, Marguerite, here
in this photograph. I know you are angry,
but bonds of blood compelled me here.
I had to see her; could not will her
into non-existence, as you do.

She should have been at Papa's funeral,
she had the right. You would not allow it.
I understand. He had another
family, one we knew nothing
about, secreted in the snowy scrub
of central Saskatchewan. These are facts.

She is thirteen. Those trips—to Ottawa,
Papa said—returning sombre,
silent, grief scoring his back, the night
the telephone rang and you answered,
but no-one replied.

You are angry, so am I. Did we
know this man? And yet. She has his clear
grey eyes, that stolid wedge of chin, scimitar
nose, sudden smile. He phoned her, the afternoon
before he died, told her he loved her.

Never once told me. In twenty years, not
once, mother, although I knew.
Such reticence left him lonely, a
planet orbiting a distant sun,
our silences a language, the body's

mute offering. But here, in these horizontal
plains, he was transformed, a man who told
his daughter she was the rain that greened

the parched and fallow fields
of his heart.

I HIDE

I hide. And wait for someone to come seek.
The game of a wounded child
in the twilight of my life.

I remember days and nights in which I'd dream
of different ways to die.
I'd try them out in my imagination:
how it would feel to walk into the sea, let the tide
carry me out, away. How it would feel, to drown:
salt water filling my nose and mouth, swelling
my lungs.

But I was too afraid, and so I carried on.
Through nightmare days and months and
years that ran together until I didn't know what
day it was, what month, what year. Only
that I was alone. Could tell no-one. Just
tremble in my silent dreams and wonder
if they were real.

Or did I just dream it all?

Then even these questions melted
into unremembering.

I was different from other children, I knew.
What could I say to them
about my world? Theirs was brightly lit
filled with homework and friends,

mothers who kissed them
goodnight. What could I say to them, these
shining girls in their white flowered dresses, in their
pink pyjamas? *"My father...   he... he...."* (But did he?)

Did he?

Even before silence had taken my tongue, sealed
my mouth, there was nothing I could say to them
which they could hear,
or hearing, understand.
Like talking to a sea bird about the life of a mole.
Incomprehensible. Unsayable. Even now.

Even now.

There is no-one left to hear my silence. To echo
its undecipherable tongue.

I hide. And wait for someone to come seek.

AUGUST 6, 1945

Borne gently in the belly of this predatory bird
I lie where a nation's hungers have hatched me.

Scientists and dreamers were midwives at my birth
and now, terror spreads its wings high above

the ocean's floor. Across the midnight sky we trace
our vector to ground zero.

Flying east, we follow the glimmering trail of sun,
as it burns its golden way across the world.

I am cradled, precious burden, in massive arms of steel.
The man whose fate it is to loose me on the world

sits silent as a corpse. Instrument of *Yomi's* fire,
Izanami's deadly work. Below us silver islands float

dreaming in dark ocean's lap. And all around, the empty sky
peels back night's temporary cloak; welcomes bloody morning.

Power of nuclear annihilation seethes in my plutonium core.
Willed to birth by human choice, I play my choiceless role.

Great arms release me from my cradle-bed. The man's voice
is broken glass. I swim down through mild blue sky

gently as a newborn slipping from the womb. And then
my pulsing heart bursts open. The explosion of my darkling star

is brighter than a million suns. And somewhere high above
the burning world a man cries out: *My God, what have we done?!*

OLDEST SON

I remember your infant rage
your fisted face bright red
mouth stretched wide and screaming.

What terrors beset you as you plunged
into life, what furies fought
inside your trembling body? I could not console you

for the losses you inherited, became
a whip of foam whirling in the maelstrom
of your anguish. You wailed, a desperate

never ending cry, pumped your tender knees hard
against your iron belly, furnace
of pain beyond my power to heal.

You beat your tiny fists against my chest, clamped
down on my nipple till it cracked
and bled, sucked peace and momentary

comfort from my body. Now you are
fifteen and slender as a wick, all that fire
transforming into incandescent beauty.

ONE WHO LIES DYING

You are dying. *I am dying.*
Are you afraid? *Not of dying, only of where it leads.*
We must talk about what it means to be led. *I am going*
                                                    soon

When I was a child . . . *You were beautiful.*
You would come to me at night . . . *like the first rain*
You would come to me, do you remember?
                              I remember your mother
in the night, you would come . . . *I can't breathe*
in the night   this is important *Help me I can't breathe*
in the dark   you would tell me
                    I've been good, I've led a blameless life
I will tell you the story *Oh yes*
of a blameless life.

Once upon a time
                        That is   the best beginning.
in the Life before life
there was an angel.
                        Ahhhhh

He lived, as angels do, in the round reach
of the Sacred. And every day
he asked the Beloved a single question:
how may I serve you? Tell me your will, and I
will make it so

And each day, the Beloved replied: *Wait. I have a*
task for you, but it is not yet time

So the angel waited, with unending
patience, readying himself for the moment
when God had need of him

This went on for an infinity of days
for in the Life before life, time is but a
stream singing
in the ocean of eternity

> *Yes, child   I know*
> *this is so*

Until one morning, when the angel asked again
God replied: *It is time*

And eagerly the angel cried: *Tell me*
Beloved, what would you have me do?

And God said to the angel: *I want you to go*
to the planet Earth, to be born there
as a male child. You know life
on this small clay planet
is a sacred privilege

> *a   sacred privilege*
> *I had forgotten*

There is a soul yet to be born
whose work it will be to delve
deep in the womb of the earth

and to bring forth, from within
its gravity, the light
of the stars. She will bear this radiance

from innermost dark
and Love will flower
in its illumination.

God asked the angel: *Do you love me enough*
to become the darkness
for this soul?

The angel bowed his head
and replied: *Whatever you want of me*
I will gladly do. Show me
where you want me to go, and I
will go

                              Ahh, my child

Then God whispered in the angel's ear
the time and place of his
birth on Earth

and said to the angel: *She will be born*
as your child, and you will serve her
by becoming darkness for her

Through you, she will bring
remembrance to those who have forgotten my face

                              Forgive me, child

And God embraced the angel, saying:
Only one who loves me as you do

would take on a form so dark, that my light
may shine in the heart of the Earth

Know this: when you go there, you will forget
you are a great angel, and loved by me

Every cell of your body will become
a prison of stone whose weight
will bear you to the bottom of the deep

And the angel replied: *Beloved*
your will
is my joy

                              Ahhhh Beloved

God placed a finger in the angel's mouth,
filling it with sweetness, and said:

When your heart is most desolate, listen
to the songs of wild places and flowing

waters. You will hear me
in the creaking of trees, in the burrowing
of moles. Rivers and streams

sing of my love. The swift breath of children
the stillness of ponds, are murmurs

of my heart. Wild geese will carry my call
snow and rain wash down
my blessing. When fires burn, listen

in the leaping, crackling flames
my voice in your ear, saying:
Beloved one, you serve me well

Beloved   I am coming
home

LAST SUPPER

We're invited to a farewell dinner
for John's stomach. Saturday night,
adults only. Next week

he has surgery for stomach cancer.
This weekend we'll feast.
Fine wine, laughter, the family gathered

around his dinner table—
John in his ceremonial kilt seated at the head.
If the cancer's spread

they'll close him up
and send him home. Two months
they say, maybe less.

This weekend
we'll feast on haggis.

THE YEAR YOU TURNED THIRTEEN

1

I remember you, the year you turned
thirteen: your long neck a slender stem;
your head hung down: a heavy,
doleful blossom.

Your hair—a dark, curly cloud
you harboured in a braid; forehead
round and candid; tender mouth full
of stones and silence.

The cliffs and ragged mountains of your life
were mirrored in the silent depths
of dreaming brown eyes
that sloped downward at the edges.

Weekday mornings you crept
past your mother's room, listened for her
snore, that spoke to you momentarily
of safety from the rabid rage that seethed,

in her blood, that glowed crimson
in the crack beneath her door.
Your feet stepped
to the rhythm of your heart.

You put on your starched white
uniform, white socks, freshly
Blancoed shoes; tiptoed
down the hall. Your school bag, heavy
with books on your shoulder;

you opened
the front door—whose hinges
you oiled each day—listened.

You slipped out of that
sleeping house, raced

down the stairs and out, into sunshine,
the noise and dust and clatter
of Unafraid.

2

The bus that carried you
to school transported you into Euclidian
order: neat lines of girls filing
into assembly, immaculate

equations, all things balanced, nothing
overweighed. Only Shakespeare, four hundred
years distant, knew
the darkness of your days.

One afternoon at recess you told
your best friend (your voice twisted
with shame): *My mother is
insane. She comes into my room*

*at night, presses her pillow
on my face. Can't breathe. So
scared, I wet my bed. Last night I
woke. She had a kitchen knife*

against my throat. . . . You faltered
in the silence. Your friend's mouth puckered
with distaste*: Don't tell such
lies about your mother,* she replied,

then turned and walked
away.

Solitary child, I remember this. You were
forsaken, and yet
faithful as an underground stream; you
wound your way through

barren mountains, steep gorges, burning
plains. All the lurid fires of that
withering time could not desiccate the flow of you.
And somehow from that parched and purple

girlhood you emerged, a muddy
child with radiant hands.

AVIARY

1

Before you were conceived your father and I
sat beside the hissing Pacific
ocean, spoke our fears:
I'm too old to stay up nights, I said,
my hair is grey;
but a seagull dropped its feather on my lap
and we surrendered

asked the One
to send us the one meant for us,
took our hearts from their bony
cages, opened them to Love. And in that moment
you were present, so radiant we grew
instantly afraid. *How can we parent a soul*
so wise, loving and joyous beyond anything we know?
And God laughed,
love filled us.
That night, tender
as earth, we made
you.

When you were born, your eyes were dark,
luminous as the night sky.
You looked deeply into everyone.
They saw in you their own
reflected hearts.
Some wept. Others glowed
as though a candle had been lit
inside.

You are ten now, wiser
than my doubts.
You have never forgotten who you are,
where you came from.
But in ten years I've watched you take
the grief of everyone and hold it
to your slender body.

You are father
to your father and to your brothers.
They lay their heads in your narrow lap. You
stroke away their fears.

I say to you now: *Be child.*
God is the sunlight, the glistening grass outside.
God is the dirt and the overarching sky.
Go ride your bike, play with friends,
enjoy. You grin, pull on your boots,
run out the front door, arms
flung wide.

2

You knock on my study door—
I know it's you, no-one else ever
knocks—and wait for me to answer.
Come in, I call. Your face appears.
Round moon face, dark almond eyes
enquiring: *are you finished yet?*
Can you come play with me?
Your pyjama top is rumpled
and your belly button shows
(when did you grow so tall?)
your wrists like birds, your fingers
knead your belly. You laugh:
I'm fat, fat, fat!

When you were two and already so
self-contained, you would gather up
your world: bottle, blanket, teddy bear,
climb into my lap, bring
your treasures with you,
put your bottle in your mouth
and close your eyes and smile and
suck and dream.

3

We were sitting on the couch last night
watching a movie when you said:
I want to do something for you. What
would you like?
You massaged my feet with peppermint cream.
Your hands were warm.
In my dreams that night
I was a wild duck resting on a moonlit pond
among a bed of rustling reeds.

FATHER

You were blind for a whole
year when you were only
eleven. Your sister told me. You never
spoke of it. She didn't know why
it happened   or how
your long dark ended. Were you
afraid?

You always wore thick
glasses, lenses tinted against
the light. Underneath,
your eyes were rabbit-shy,
so timid I wanted to shelter you
in my arms, keep you
safe from harm. Now I remember
all the ways you hid. How you refused to see
what you could not
heal. My mother's
madness, the way you both
abandoned my sister at birth,
an unwanted
gift. You closed your eyes.
Now I,

your unflinching daughter, hold
the sun in both
hands, carry its
illumination. I want nothing
hidden, demand
to see all, search every
shadow for its private
vision. This
is your blind legacy, Daddy.

TRANSPLANT

We've waited a long time for this appointment.
Two months, at least, since you
called me from the Emergency Room
on my birthday. *I've had*
blood tests and ultrasounds, you said,
now they want an ECG.

You came home. Your face was grey.
Your eyes, yellow in the lingering light,
were innocent as rain. I want details.
Names, diagnoses. You cannot tell me.
When you're tired, scared, you can't
remember, not even the important things.
I clench my mouth, reach for tenderness and find
a prickly pear   a spear   a hedgehog hair.
I find such boiling anger in my tears.

And now we're here. The waiting
room is bright. Orange chairs and racks
of magazines. The air is hot and stale.
You are tired from the trip,
the ferry ride across the water,
the long drive from Horseshoe Bay.
We have not talked; your eyes
a question mine avoid.

The doctor is young: cheerful, scrubbed, clinically
detached. His voice a scalpel; something
clean, sharp-edged, but ultimately kind.

Cirrhosis, he tells us, breezy as a zephyr.
Your liver hardened
like an attitude. Hepatitis C swarming
in your blood, destroying organs, cells,
shrivelling your liver, ballooning
your spleen. *No cure*, he trumpets, big
teeth gleaming as he smiles. *Go home. Wait
till you get sicker. You' re going to need
a transplant, a whole new liver.*
How long, I ask, wanting to hear
the worst of it. The doctor's voice lilts as he
delivers his statistics: *Twenty per cent die
without ever receiving an organ.*
(I watch your mouth, flat as a counterpane)
*After the transplant, eighty per cent still alive
within a year; sixty per cent in five years.*

I look at you. You had a haircut yesterday.
In light of what we've heard this seems
utterly profligate. Sixty per cent.
What would they take? Your shadowed
face, round, brown eyes, twisty curling
hair, your stubby-fingered hands.
Deeper. Liver, kidney, spleen—your
dark insides. What's left? Pumping
heart and lungs, fretwork of nerves,
bony cased brain. What makes a you?
Your voice of melted earth, bent
humour, your hockey-loving soul.

We drive to Horseshoe Bay, eat at Troll's,
talk slowly between sips of soup. *I'm scared*,
you say. I cup your pounding pulse in the hollow
of my hand. You are not my child. I do not know
how to comfort you, how to say: *rest in Eternity's lap.*
You either know this, or you don't.
And I have always known.

Waves of our history sweep from your shore
to mine. We have children, we have lives
that intertwine. In this moment I don't know
what love is. I know danger, anger, fear;
the missed step, the solitary ear. But love
without need—only God is so vulnerable;
posts no guards, defends no territory, does not
bully, plead, threaten, cajole, take a stand
as we do, you and I.

God's vulnerability I understand
and pray to emulate. Now
I tremble at the brink I have invoked.

Small children cower in my belly,
fierce voices rage. I brace the tide.

HUSBAND

Eighteen months since you were diagnosed,
a failing liver. So tired,
this afternoon you could not make it
to your bed, stumbled to my study
trembling like a tree
about to crash. I led you
ungently by the hand, smoothed out
your sheets, untwisted pillows while you
yanked at my arm, impatient to lie down.

I am widowed by that part of you already gone
your body burned away by toxic
waste, debris drifting darkly
into upper regions of your brain, starving
it of oxygen. You forget things, where you put
your address book, what day this is.
Whole sentences disappear
while you hold doggedly
to a shred of thought that remains
unborn.

I miss you. You
are too ill to care, need more
than I can give, urgent mouth sucking
on the electronic breast of television
in the dim cave
of your room. You have turned away
in your shrinking world, to all but
your decaying body.

There is more to love than simple commerce,
giving and receiving. Yet the deepest well
runs dry
in prolonged absence of rain.

I am tired.
My body is stretched thin, the skin
of some exotic animal curved taut
over a drumbeat.

BLESSINGS

Seeds round with blessings breathe
and ripen in my womb

Bless me with listening, so your words
become the visible, dancing
shape of my being

Bless me with patience, to enter
the timing
of your perfect rhythm

Bless me with courage, undisturbed
by shadows. Let my soul bind the stalks
of my scattered selves into golden stooks

Bless me with humour, that I may dance
lightly on earth, breezes of
laughter springing under my feet

As the deer's velvet muzzle finds nourishment
in thorny thickets,
bless me with gentleness

Bless me with desire, that my longing
may lead me to you

My heart
radiates your peace,
my mind
mirrors your grace,
your wisdom's river
flows through my life

Bless me with the clarity
of well-water, the truth
of fire, the patience
of earth, swift mutability
of air

Ancient clay of my body,
may these seeds be
nurtured to fruition in my life—

your germ is born in me to bless
this sacred soil, my home

YOU

Your blessings have flowed down
like rain upon these pages.

Your voice in my throat, your words
flowing from my fingertips.

You take my stubborn smallness
and stretch me into eternity.

You the ruby blood that
surges in my heart.

You, Beloved, you.

MOTHER

I speak of you last, you who remain
the epicentre of my life.
Your sins of omission narrow down to one:

you did not love me.
How long must I condemn myself for that?
All those nights you prowled

through my room dreaming up fresh tortures
for your delectation, your smile
a rictus as you wrapped your hands

around my throat, choking out the life
you once bestowed. I was innocent of all but
longing for you. I have looked for you

in men who could not love me,
abandonment familiar as the taste of yearning
in my mouth. You were dead

many years before I stopped groping
towards you, blind moth
to the mother-flame.

FLIGHT TO FREEDOM

My ancestors launched into the Arabian Sea
in tiny coracles fragile as leaves
to escape the *jihad*.

Their country
overrun by Arab invaders, their people
slaughtered in the name of Allah,

they entrusted their bodies to the tides,
sailed east to India; fled
for their lives and for freedom to worship

Ahura Mazda, the god
of their ancestors. The year
was 760 AD.

Thirteen hundred years later, I take flight
westward across that churning sea.
Seeds of their spirit

in me. Those ancestors,
with their wandering blood, keep me questing,
peregrine.

I do not own the comforts
of their religion, seek instead a god

who lives in me; am impelled,
not by raiders but
by this spirit's urgent embarkation

to be free.

About the Author

Hiro Boga was born in Bombay in 1949 and moved to the west coast of Canada in 1976. She now lives with her son in Nanaimo, BC. She holds an MFA in Creative Writing from the University of British Columbia, where she was a University Graduate Fellow from 2000 to 2002. She has twice received BC Arts Council Awards, and has been a finalist in the CBC Literary Awards. Her novel, *Shahnaz,* was published in Canada by Oolichan Books in 2000 and released by Penguin on the Indian subcontinent in 2002.